Delusion
and
God's Salvation

Other Books by the Author

The Coming End of the Age

An Overview of the Endtime

Preparing For the Lord's Return

Greapa

The Coming of the King in Matthew 24 and 25

The Goal and Peak of Our Christian Experience
Insights into Revelation, Book 1

The Beast, His Image, and His Mark
Insights into Revelation, Book 2

Firstfruits and Harvest
Insights into Revelation, Book 3

A Place Prepared
Insights into Revelation, Book 4

The Church in Philadelphia
Insights into Revelation, Book 5

A Faithful God

Booklets by the Author

The Heart of God	The Rapture
The Heart of God II	Urgency or Complacency
The Heart of God III	A New Creation
The Heart of God IV	The Spirit
The Heart of God V	The Spirit Was Not Yet
The Heart of God VI	The Lark Ascending
Redemption and Salvation	The Order of Melchizedek
Signs of the End	The Prayer of the End

Visit **aplaceinthewilderness.com** for more about these books (including their introduction, table of contents, and ordering information) and booklets.

Delusion
and
God's Salvation

Paul Cozza

A Place in the Wilderness

Delusion and God's Salvation

© 2018 Paul Cozza

ISBN 978-1-5136-3777-8

All rights reserved.
No part of this publication may be reproduced or transmitted in any form or by any means—electronic, mechanical, or any other, including photocopy, recording, or any information or retrieval system—without prior written consent, in hardcopy paper form, from:

Paul Cozza
A Place in the Wilderness

Website: aplaceinthewilderness.com
Email: paul@aplaceinthewilderness.com

Second printing: July, 2025

Scripture quotations are from the American Standard Version of the Bible (1901) unless otherwise noted.

Cover design: Nuggitz Creative Services (Nuggitz.com)
Cover image: © bychykhin | DepositPhotos.com

Table of Contents

Introduction 1
  Hasty Judgment 1
  Clandestine Agendas 4
  Something More Serious 4
  A Christian Solution 5

Chapter 1 – Delusion Described 7
  Imagination 7
  Fantasy 8
  Delusion 9
  Foundational 9
  The Self 10
  The Source 10
  Character Flaws 11
  Separation 11

Chapter 2 – Delusion Exemplified 13
  Atheists 13
  Evolutionists 14
  Religionists 14
  Job 16
  Saul 17
  The Many 18
  The Church in Laodicea 19
  Satan 19

Chapter 3 – Delusion Rectified 23
  Job 24
  Saul 25
  The Crucial Factor 27
  Prayer 28

Appendix – The Case of James **31**
   His Upbringing *31*
   An Unbeliever *32*
   Christ's Appearing *32*
   In Jerusalem *32*
   His Writings *33*
   His Martyrdom *33*
   Analysis *33*
   In Summary *36*

Note to the reader
Explanations and further details about the text appear as footnotes. Scripture references are cited in the numbered **References** list at the end of each chapter.

Introduction

I am not a clinical psychologist. However, since becoming a Christian I have been a student of human behavior. I have not been a student in the sense of attending courses at a university. Rather, I have been a student by observing human behavior and seeking to understand why people act the way they do. Much of what I have observed has been of myself, as often understanding and dealing with the self is paramount to spiritual growth. But I've also spent much time observing and considering others. By coming to a true and genuine understanding of the condition of others, we are better able to pray for them and afford them help if the need should arise.

I've been a Christian since the early 1970s and over time I've reach some conclusions about human behavior. While the conclusions are general in nature, they are applicable to just about everyone to one degree or another, for we all suffer from the human condition! It does not matter whether we have been born again or not. We all are susceptible to the same psychological "diseases." Simply being a Christian does not immunize us to these psychological problems. In fact, these inner afflictions may be harsher and more intense, since Satan, God's enemy, considers it quite a prize to damage God's people.

Hasty Judgment

One such psychological problem that I have observed somewhat frequently is hasty judgment – forming an opinion after having heard or read about only part or one side of a situation. This is to come to a conclusion without having all the facts, and perhaps having only biased information. Evidently, this is a fairly common problem, for the Bible enjoins us to require two witnesses before judgment is pronounced.[1] In addition, Peter warns us about coming to an understanding of a portion of the Bible apart from its context and from the Bible as a whole, saying that no Scripture is of private interpretation.[2] That is to say, no verse can be interpreted by itself. Doing so can lead to one's own destruction[3] and serious damage to others.

This particular problem arises often in personal relationships. One may hear a particular version of a story and come to a conclusion based on that without ever having heard the other side of that story. A person may pronounce judgment upon another without ever having spoken to or heard from the one being so judged! Such behavior is bad enough when what is heard comes from someone involved in the situation. But it is far worse when it is based upon unsubstantiated gossip being passed from one to another.

Let me give an example. One day I was invited to lunch by a young brother in the Lord. As we were completing our meal, this brother brought up a much older servant of the Lord, and told me that this older one had been promoting heresy. I knew this older servant fairly well and did not receive such an accusation easily or lightly. Rather, I asked this young brother what the heresy was that this older servant was promoting. The young one told me that he didn't know. I responded that if he didn't know for himself what the heresy was he should not be speaking such words. He then replied that he was "just following the brothers." That is to say, he had been told by others that a heresy was being promoted and without ever having checked the veracity of such a claim, this younger one was then spreading this slanderous[*] accusation, thinking that what he was doing was something of God.

How can we Christians behave in such a base and ungodly fashion? How can we slander others and yet pride ourselves in our "good works?" There are a number of factors involved in such behavior. From a spiritual perspective, there is a lack of that genuine prayer which touches God. Such prayer brings us into God's heart and mind, calms and warns us, and illuminates us regarding both the one-sidedness of what we think we know and the possible problems with our understanding of matters.

From a psychological perspective, this could be caused by any of a number of problems. Often those who are quick to judge

---

[*] According to my understanding of this accusation, it was absurd on its face, and was made by some who sought to rid themselves of an older brother who would not conform to their ways – a very dark situation indeed!

have untrained minds. That is, they have never been properly disciplined to evaluate all aspects of a situation before coming to a conclusion. They may believe what they hear simply because it is the first thing they have heard. This was Eve's problem in the garden. She heard something from Satan, believed it, and then acted upon it without ever considering alternatives or speaking with her spouse, Adam. A trained mind does not jump to conclusions or judgments.

As a counter-example, consider the Beroeans in the book of Acts.[4] They received the word of Paul with readiness of mind, and examined the scriptures daily to see if what Paul spoke was in accordance with them. This demonstrated not only a disciplined mind but also a proper spirit toward God.

Hasty judgment may also be due to misplaced faith. We might place our faith in other human beings, believing that they can be trusted, that they would never hurt us, that they are godly and we should therefore follow them. This is misplaced faith. Every human being is susceptible to errors of all kinds – errors in judgment, errors in behavior, errors through biases, errors through motives. The list of our possible errors is seemingly endless. To blindly follow others is to invite disaster. Our faith must be in God and God alone. Furthermore, we follow others only as much as they follow Christ. If they deviate from Christ, we must not follow them in their error.

Another source of this problem is unrestrained emotions. Sometimes we may hear something that stirs us up, enflames our emotions. Without taking the time to calm ourselves and consider the situation properly, we may act upon what we have heard, or at least accept what we've heard as true. Our emotions must be calm and restrained, never ruling us or our actions.

An additional factor that can result in quick judgment is hidden bias. Within us we may be prejudiced against someone for one reason or another. When we hear something negative about him or her, we may accept such an accusation not because it is true, not because we have verified it, and not for any reason other than we *want* it to be true because of our bias. This is a serious problem and, if left untouched, will eventually taint all that we are and all that we do.

Clandestine Agendas

A second psychological problem that seems fairly common is clandestine agendas. Often people have an inward intention, with some goal or goals they seek to accomplish. This motivates them to act in a certain way. While they may be outwardly presenting themselves in one manner, their hidden motives compel them to act in another. Whether their motives are bad or good in their own eyes is immaterial – having *any* agenda, having any motive is impure. As Christians our only reason for acting is Christ Himself. He, the living Person, is our motivating factor. To have any other motivation in our hearts is impure.

Often the hidden intention is to promote oneself or one's cause. Similarly, the intention may be to bring down others. In the eyes of the one so acting, what he or she is doing is good and needed. However, this behavior causes great damage.

Having such a clandestine agenda can cause a person to act peculiarly, even in a bizarre fashion. One may purport to be speaking forth God's word, and yet when a hidden agenda is at work, what is stated may blatantly contradict the Bible. Outlandish statements and actions, absurd and foolish, may be the result. Beware of clandestine agendas.

Something More Serious

There is yet another, more serious psychological problem, one that is the subject of this book. It is something that has caused great difficulty and concern to me in my life. At times throughout the years I have encountered behavior that I simply could not understand, no matter how I looked at it. There was no way to reason with the person in question. When contradicted, the person would refuse to let go of what they believed to be true. Even when directly told their perception was not real, they still held on to that which was not true. At times I have seen people fabricate things that were not only untrue, but *could not* be true. Yet the ones behaving in this way firmly believed what they were saying was factual. Such behavior left me dumbfounded. I had no explanation for it, no understanding of it, and no means of dealing with it.

One day a friend mentioned the word delusion. I began to consider whether such a term was applicable to those cases I had encountered. I started to research the term and the typical manifestations of a delusional state. What I had been experiencing and had found inexplicable fit very well with delusion.

As I was working on a seemingly unrelated book a few months ago, a whole section on delusion came forth. I was quite surprised, and had no idea how this section was going to fit into the book on which I was working. It was not until I was nearing its completion that I saw the importance of that portion.

Then, as I prayed one morning a few days later I felt from the Lord that He had more to say. This is such a serious and important topic that it needed to be addressed with a whole book. This must be a matter on the Lord's heart.

A Christian Solution

Finally, as implied by its title, this book is specifically written for Christians. As genuine Christians believe and know, Christ is the reality, the truth. Apart from Him everything is false; apart from Him all is delusion. And so, the only true salvation from a delusional state is a Christian matter.

References

[1] Deut. 19:15; Matt. 18:16; 2 Cor. 13:1; 1 Tim. 5:19
[2] 2 Pet. 1:20
[3] 2 Pet. 3:16
[4] Acts 17:10-11

CHAPTER 1

Delusion Described

Delusion is a condition of the mind and heart, a state of being in which deception rules. It is not just a matter of being deceived – we all suffer from being deceived to some level. Rather, when deception rules the heart, when deception becomes the norm, when a lie is accepted as the truth and held onto at all costs, when the lie is woven into the fabric of a person's character, that is delusion.

Delusion does not happen quickly. It is not an overnight occurrence. It evolves over many years and through various stages. It takes quite some time for deception to infiltrate the various parts of a person's character and insidiously control perceptions.

Imagination

Delusion begins with the imagination. In and of itself the imagination is a good thing, something of God's creation. It allows us to transcend the limits of our past experiences and our knowledge. It motivates us to explore that which is unknown. A healthy imagination is an extremely valuable asset. Consider what the human race would be like without imagination. There would be little if any invention, exploration, and progression. Mankind would stagnate.

However, an unbridled imagination is problematic. It can become a breeding ground of deception and misdirection. Such an imagination is fertile soil for evil influences and malevolent concepts. How many evil devices, physical or otherwise, have been spawned in the imagination of man? How many immoral deeds have germinated in man's imagination? An unconstrained imagination is easily influenced and used by Satan. The injection of the "right" thought at a particular moment can lead to all kinds of damage and destruction.

It is here in the imagination that delusion starts. For those who are especially gifted in some way, their imaginations may begin to consider themselves special because of these gifts. To the one who has suffered trauma or abuse of some sort, the imagination may consider that mistreatment ongoing, when in fact it no longer exists. To the one who is searching for an escape from some unbearable or perhaps simply unpalatable situation, the imagination may construct an alternative reality. In all these cases, the unconstrained imagination dwells upon something unreal, something false, and through such a continual conversation with deception, causes what is unreal to grow and thrive within.

Fantasy

Over time what began as imagination may give way to fantasy. By this I do not mean the typical fantasies in which we probably all have indulged at one point or another in our lives, particularly in our youth. Rather, I am referring to skewed perception, where our view of the world around us and particularly of ourselves in that world is not according to fact. While we all to one degree or another have a skewed perception of ourselves, in this stage of the delusion's development, one lives in a perceptual realm that is unreal. What was once imagined is now believed to be true. It is imagination coupled with falsehood and deception, and then allowed to make its home in the heart. That which was once imagined has become a kind of manufactured inward reality. The fantasy is believed to be true and real, but it is not.

At this point, if the inward fantasy is contradicted by outward happenings and facts, the fantasy is overthrown and discarded. Its hold upon the individual is not yet so strong as to override reality when that reality controverts the fantasy. The belief in the fantasy may be strong but is not yet overpowering, and it is still possible for the whole fabricated structure within to be brought down with the truth.

However, if the fantasy is allowed to continue unchecked, and if the inward deception is not exposed and the causal factors are not dealt with, it can lead to a far worse condition, something much more difficult to rectify.

Delusion

Over time what was merely fantasy can become a delusion. While a fantasy can be undone by truth, facts, and contradicting evidence, this is not the case with a delusion. A fantasizer will let go of their fantasy when confronted with that which proves it to be false. One who is deluded does not let go of the delusion. Such a one will deny the truth, twist facts, and ignore evidence in order to maintain the delusion. When confronted with something that is contrary to the fabricated internal realm in which the deluded one lives, he will ignore the contradiction rather than examine it and allow the truth to penetrate and change him.

One suffering from delusion may act normally a good portion of the time. He may be able to perform daily tasks normally, converse with others without any noticeable problem, and carry out any number of undertakings as would be expected. But when the right circumstances arise, the delusion is manifested, and the one suffering from it may appear to almost have a separate personality. They can then behave in a most peculiar and bizarre fashion, very different from what is typical for them.

Once a person is deluded it is extraordinarily difficult to rescue them from the delusion. Extreme measures become necessary, but they are no guarantee that the delusion will cease in a timely fashion.

Foundational

Delusion is a serious inward foundational deception so entrenched in the personality as to become part of the person. Once fantasy has become delusion, it is part of the character, part of the very person. It has become a foundation-stone of the personality. It may be the main basis upon which the whole personality rests. And, like some kind of insidious mold, it will slowly creep into and affect nearly every aspect of the person. While at times such a one may appear normal, lurking there under the surface is the ever present delusion.

The one suffering from this condition will hold onto the delusion at all costs, because removal of it would mean the uprooting and collapse of the whole personality built upon it. Furthermore, in some cases there may be underlying issues that the delusion was invented to avoid. Removing the delusion would mean confronting those seemingly unbearable issues.

The Self

Delusion is centered on the self, based in the self, and actually part of the self.* The self seems to always be centrally involved in delusion. Often the delusion involves self-exaltation, or at times self-abasement, self-indulgence, or self-flagellation. But, it always has to do with the self. For good or bad, in the delusion the self is the center of the universe. Delusion turns one's consciousness and awareness inward, focusing it on the self. Eventually that self becomes the universe in which the deluded one lives.

The Source

Every delusion is a lie. Every lie has its source in the evil one, Satan, the father of lies.¹ And, as we will see, he brings about delusions with a particular evil intent.

A delusion may have an element of truth unit. There may have been some trauma, abuse, or suffering in a person's life that forms the core of a delusion. Alternatively, there may have been some great success or achievement, or some notable talent that lies at the core. However, in the delusion that truth is always twisted and then exaggerated. It seems to take on a life of its own, existing outside of time and space. The truth that once was no longer is, yet the deluded one still sees it as being present. If the delusion has to do with a person, that person who is no longer present still appears to be. The deluded one still believes that person to be near in one form or another. This is all the evil one's working to blind and entrap.

All of this has an inflating effect within the deluded one. Small, minor, and trivial things can be magnified, becoming enormously important and significant, causing unpredictable and disproportionate reactions. Happenings completely unrelated to a

---

* By the "self," I mean the person of the fallen human being. It is the human person apart from Christ, the unregenerated human being, the "old man." When we are born again, we still continue to experience our self. It is eliminated slowly over time, as Christ grows within us and gains our heart.

person may conjure up past feelings, resulting in greatly exaggerated responses. All this is from the evil one's working and operation.

Character Flaws

Often the evil one will use character flaws to bring about a delusion. A character flaw can be a doorway for the entry of a lie. The flaw can then become the residing place for the disease of delusion to grow and thrive. Eventually it can become delusion's home.

For example, the proud might imagine themselves to be higher or greater then they are. Their character flaw – pride – becomes the entryway for a lie about their proper station in life. Eventually, their delusion of greatness resides in that pride.

Similarly, the ones who are insecure might imagine themselves to be under constant attack. Childish ones might be accustomed to having their way, and therefore consider themselves special and deserving. In all these cases it is the character flaw that is the fertile soil for the seed, growth, and maturation of delusion.

Separation

Satan's intention is to ensnare and keep a person imprisoned within the delusion. Eventually one so afflicted is enslaved in and to that lie, constantly being forced to twist, contradict, ignore, avoid, and bury the truth in order to maintain that delusion.

Much more importantly, on a deeper level, Satan's desire is to keep man separated from God. This is Satan's ultimate goal – separation from Christ.[*] This is the most significant aspect of his operation in delusion.

---

[*] It may be that "Christ" even plays a part in the delusion. Yet, as we will see, that is also a lie. Christ Himself, His very Person, is truth, reality. A lie cannot exist in His presence. So if there is a delusion, Christ Himself is not part of it. One might imagine that he is serving Christ or doing God's will, but this is false and simply part of the deluded person's inner fabrication.

References

[1] Jn. 8:44

CHAPTER 2

Delusion Exemplified

If we consider in the light of God's Word the condition of man, the billions of people on the earth, and the world about us that man has constructed, we come to an inescapable conclusion: to one degree or another, and in one form or another, there is delusion virtually everywhere.

Recall what the apostle John said – the whole world lies in the evil one.[1] John had certainly been delivered from all delusion when he wrote his epistles. His fellowship was with the Father and with His Son, Jesus Christ.[2] In such a fellowship any and all delusions that John might have had at one time were gone. John's self had been dealt with. He was a person in Christ. What he saw was truth, reality. And he told us that the whole world lies in the evil one. This was the frank assessment and vision of an elderly brother and apostle in the Lord.

How many people of the billions that live today see this reality? Hardly any. Even among Christians, very few see the world for what it is. Why is this? Because delusion is everywhere. Satan has fashioned this world to blind and entrap man. Through delusion he has captured nearly everyone. It is only God's mercy and working within man that has delivered, and is delivering, some from this world's delusion.

Atheists

There are many who declare there is no God.* Those that actually believe this are not only greatly deceived, but totally deluded. We know there is a God. Christians know Him personally, experiencing Him daily.

---

* I once was such a one, an avowed atheist. How amazing that Grace that saved a wretch like me!

Furthermore, the whole creation declares God. In order to accept the notion that there is no God, what the very senses shout out must be ignored. And, in order to maintain the delusion, atheists must reject everything that declares God to them.

Many of these hate the God whom they say doesn't exist, and do their utmost to eradicate every recognition of God from the earth. They are unable to contact the divine Spirit because of their condition, and so absurdly deny His existence. This is similar to a blind person* denying the existence of color.

This is all great delusion, and everyone who truly believes there is no God is either greatly deluded or a deceiver trying to deceive and delude others.

Evolutionists

Let us turn to those who state that evolution is a fact. These too are deluded. In an effort to deny the existence of God they propose an impossible theory, and then declare the theory fact. These, who imagine themselves to be genuine and proper scientists, ignore the very mathematics upon which science is based, mathematics which proves their theory absolutely impossible. When confronted with such mathematics, their response is that the mathematics must be wrong, because they know evolution is true. What is this? This is not the response of the scientist. Rather, this is the typical response of denial given by one who is deluded.

Given the probabilities associated with the construction of long strands of DNA, the probability of evolution, as set forth by current theory, having occurred by random chance is so far-fetched as to be ludicrous. Nevertheless, evolutionists ignore these facts in order to maintain their theory. Why is this? They are deluded.

Religionists

Let me preface this section by giving a definition of religion. Religion is man's attempt to worship God without Christ

---

* Or, perhaps more like a person who refuses to open his eyes.

and apart from Christ. Consider the story of Cain and Abel. In Genesis Abel offered of the firstlings of the flock to God.[3] This was according to the way God had set up when he slayed an animal and covered Adam and Eve with its skin.[4] This was a type of Christ, of what He would do on the cross, and of what He was to be to His people. Abel's offering of a lamb from the flock was his acceptance of God's way and of Christ. As a consequence, God received Abel's offering.

On the other hand, Cain offered of the fruit of the ground to God. This was Cain rejecting God's way and, in type, rejecting Christ. Cain was offering God something that came forth from himself, never acknowledging that he was a fallen human being, had sin dwelling within him, and was therefore corrupted. God would not and could not accept such an offering and consequently rejected it. The proof of the corruption hidden within Cain and his offering was that he later murdered his brother, revealing what was in his heart all along.

What Cain did in offering something to God apart from God's way was the beginning of religion. That religion has grown and blossomed into all the religions we now see upon the face of the earth, every one of which attempts to worship God without Christ.

Consider the Muslims. They believe that God exists. They call Him Allah. They attempt to worship their God in prayer. However, they deny Christ. They deny that Jesus is God become a man. They deny His work of redemption on the cross. They deny that He is the way to God. There is one massive problem with their beliefs – Christ is the *only* way to God. When Christ declared that no one comes to the Father except through Him,[5] He revealed that everything else, every other attempt to worship God, any means of worship apart from Him is false. What then is the result of giving oneself over to this kind of falsehood? Delusion.

Muslims believe that they can somehow be accepted by God without Christ. This is a delusion. They do not see the depth of corruption within man and within themselves. Were they to see this, to face this reality, they would cry out for the deliverance that only Christ Himself can provide.

What is the result of their delusion? They* hate Israel, who are God's earthly people. They hate Christians, who are God's heavenly people. We also see vile acts of terrorism and murder in the name of their God. What does this tell us? They are deluded to the point of insanity, thinking that God condones and accepts such abhorrent behavior.

Job

There are various examples of delusion in the Bible. Although it is not called that by name, the fact is there. It can be found in both the Old and New Testaments, among men and angels, and in both Jews and Christians. It seems that no higher life form is immune to delusion. Only God Himself, who is the reality, cannot be deluded.

Consider Job in the Old Testament, who is perhaps the premier example of delusion. Most readers of the book of Job consider his experience to have been a test of his patience. After all, Job was perfect and upright. He had perfected his human living. Even God said he was perfect and shunned evil.[6] What could possibly have been wrong with Job?

However, the idea that God was proving Job's patience is a misconception,† an error that obscures what was really happening in God's dealings with Job. What so many fail to see when they read this book is that Job had a huge problem, one that required extreme measures to resolve. Over time, as Job perfected his living, he began to believe that he was righteous. This was his view of himself – a righteous and perfect person. He said this more than once[7] in the book of Job. This is also indicated by his actions. He offered sacrifices to God on behalf of his children, thinking that they may have sinned in their hearts.[8] But there is no mention

---

* I am speaking in generalities. Not every Muslim is so filled with hatred, malice, and murder. However, as we look at the world situation today and what is occurring in it, it is evident that very many Muslims are. This is the result of their delusion.

† It is true that James, the apostle and physical brother of the Lord, spoke of Job's patience. However, I refer the reader to the Appendix on page 31, which describes the case of James in detail.

of Job offering sacrifices for himself. Evidently, he believed he had no need.

From this we can see that Job had a high opinion of himself – too high. Job's life was one centered on himself, having all to do with himself and the perfecting of himself. He was altogether wrapped up in himself. As a consequence he was apart from God; he was separated from God. The very self upon which he centered became a veil keeping him from God. In addition, because he was separated from God, he could not see his true condition, his real self.

The book of Job is not about patience or long-suffering. It is about delusion. Job was deluded, thinking he was righteous. The proof that he was deluded is at the very end of the book. There Job says that he had heard of God by the hearing of the ear, but then his eye saw God. Therefore, he abhorred himself and repented in dust and ashes.[9] When the reality shined upon Job, his delusion evaporated and Job saw his real condition. He then hated himself. Job's delusion had been dispelled and he had been saved from it.

Saul

In the New Testament consider the apostle Paul. He was originally Saul of Tarsus.[10] He was born of the tribe of Benjamin[11] and raised a Pharisee according to the strictest sect of the Jews.[12] He was taught by Gamaliel,[13] who was considered one of the greatest of Jewish teachers. Saul was a Hebrew of the Hebrews.[14]

With respect to zeal for the teachings and traditions he had learned, he persecuted the church.[15] He consented to and abetted the murder of Stephen,[16] the first martyr of the church age. He breathed out threatenings and slaughter toward Christians,[17] laying waste to the church.[18] He persecuted the brethren, punishing and imprisoning some.[19] Others he tormented, attempting to force them to blaspheme.[20] He agreed not only to the murder of Stephen, but of others as well.[21] Today such a person would be tried and imprisoned for these crimes.

Saul of Tarsus was a madman,[22] raging against Christians. He was so deluded that he had become nearly insane. He was deluded to the point of murder. He had been overtaken by what I term "religious insanity." He thought he was doing God's work.

In fact, he was persecuting God.[23] This was not merely deception. This was something far deeper and stronger – *delusion*. He was living in an unreal and false realm.

The Many

As another example, consider the many who tell the Lord at His return that they had done great works by His name. They prophesied, cast out demons, and did many other great works by His name.[24] The Lord does not dispute that they did such works; He does not rebuke them for lying. Clearly they had done such things. However, the Lord does not acknowledge them. Rather, He says he never knew them. How crucial this word is. He never *knew* them! He had no consciousness of them in their doings and in their works. All that they did was apart from Him. It was apart from the Spirit, something done on their own, without God's participation.

These are certainly Christians. They call Jesus "Lord."[25] They are speaking with Him at his return. The unbelievers aren't resurrected until a thousand years after the Lord's return. There is no question that these are genuine Christians speaking with Jesus. Yet they are deluded. They lived a grand delusion their Christian lives, believing they were working for God.

Furthermore, consider how deluded they are. They have the brazenness to actually rebuke Jesus, saying to Him, "Lord, Lord, did we not do this great work in Your Name? Did we not do that great work in Your Name? Did we not do many things in Your Name?" In essence they are telling the Lord Himself, "How can You reject us when we did so many things for You?" How brazen this is. Rather than feel shame for having lived apart from Christ after they were saved, they remonstrate with the Lord Himself. This illustrates how greatly deluded these are.

Consider all the supposed great Christian works being done today in the Lord's name and those that have been done in the past. How many of those performing such works will be among the ones the Lord described in Matthew 7? How great their shock will be when the Lord tells them, "Depart from Me, you that work lawlessness!"

The Church in Laodicea

In Revelation the Lord speaks as the Spirit to seven churches in Asia. To the church in Laodicea he says that they think they are rich and have need of nothing. However, they are poor, blind, wretched, miserable, and naked.[26] How pitiful the condition of the church in Laodicea is. The believers in this type of gathering are entirely deluded. They believe something that is completely false. They live as if they have the riches of Christ and need nothing. In reality this is totally false. The truth is the exact opposite. They are poor, having little if any riches of Christ. They are blind, not seeing their own condition and not beholding Christ. They are wretched and miserable. How pitiful they are within, not even being aware of their true inward condition. They are naked and their shame is exposed before God, not covered by the Christ whom they have shut out. They think they have need of nothing, and yet Christ is on the outside knocking to enter in. How can such people be helped, when the One that can help them is on the outside, and yet they believe He is within. This is an example of the Lord's word in Matthew, "If the light that is in you is darkness, how great is that darkness."[27]

I was in such a place for a time. More than once I heard the most prominent speaker among us liken our condition to Laodicea. However, it seemed nearly everyone was deaf to such a word. Generally, there was no desperation to be saved from that condition. For the most part there was no weeping before the Lord in repentance. There was hardly any crying out to God to be saved. Most continued as if all was fine. They could and would not accept how bad their condition was. Indeed, some mocked those who did cry out and weep. How sad this is. How deluded they have become, thinking they have need of nothing. The Lord have mercy on these dear saints.

Satan

As a final example, let us consider the angel Satan. Before his fall he was named Lucifer,[28] which means "bearer of light." And such he was. He was the highest of all the angels. Even after his fall, Michael the archangel dared not rebuke him.[29] This tells us of Lucifer's extraordinary status. He was the most intelligent, brightest, and most beautiful[30] of all God's creation. He walked in the heavenly garden of God with the Lord.[31] He was close to God, God's friend. He was a priest in God's service.

This was until evil was found in him; pride about his own beauty consumed him.[32] He thought that he could make himself like God and rule in God's stead. He thought and still thinks that he can lord it over God and enslave God to do his bidding. In this great fall the bearer of light, Lucifer, became God's adversary, Satan.

Of all of God's creatures, Satan is the most deluded. Consider: He thinks he can bring down God! He thinks he is smarter, wiser, more capable then the One who created him. How incredibly deluded he is. He knows the Bible, and knows what is written concerning him, and yet refuses to let go of his delusion. And in his case, this has led him to become the most vile, base, evil, despicable, and foul thing in existence.

References

[1] 1 Jn. 5:19
[2] 1 Jn. 1:3
[3] Gen. 4:4
[4] Gen. 3:21
[5] Jn. 14:6
[6] Job 1:8
[7] Job 6:29; 9:21; 13:18; 32:1; 34:5
[8] Job 1:5
[9] Job 42:5-6
[10] Acts 9:11; 21:39
[11] Phil. 3:5
[12] Acts 26:5
[13] Acts 22:3
[14] Phil. 3:5
[15] Phil. 3:6
[16] Acts 7:58; 8:1
[17] Acts 9:1
[18] Acts 8:3
[19] Acts 8:3
[20] Acts 26:11
[21] Acts 22:4; 26:10

[22] Acts 26:11
[23] Acts 9:4-5
[24] Matt. 7:21-23
[25] 1 Cor. 12:3
[26] Rev. 3:17
[27] Matt. 6:23
[28] Is. 14:12
[29] Jude 1:9
[30] Ez. 28:17
[31] Ez. 28:12-15
[32] Ez. 28:15; Is. 14:13-14

CHAPTER 3

Delusion Rectified

When deception is so deep that it is woven into a person's character, how is it possible to cure that? When the very foundation of a person's character is at least in part a lie, what can be done? In fact, there is no cure. Nothing can be done. It is not possible to truly heal such a condition.

Except by death! A dead deluded person no longer poses a problem. The only way to help one suffering from such a condition is death, the death of the cross – being crucified with Christ.*

Knowing that man was incurably infected with sin, and that the indwelling sinful nature would inflict damage of all kinds within man, God has provided a marvelous solution. On the cross as Christ died we all died with Him.[1] And, when Christ rose from the grave in resurrection, we rose with Him.[2] Our self, our old man, that diseased old person that we were, died with Christ[3] and was left in the grave. In His resurrection we are born again[4] as a new creation,[5] a new person, a son of God. This is God's provision to save us from delusion.

How is the cross of Christ and Christ's resurrection worked out in us experientially? Christ's death and resurrection and their application to us are divine, eternal facts. However, working those facts into our experience takes time, God's operation within us, and our cooperation. How is it possible for us to die on the cross, and yet live in resurrection experientially? To understand this, let us consider some examples in the Bible of God's dealing with delusion through the application of Christ's death and resurrection.

---

* In fact, the death of our old man in Christ on the cross is the cure for every condition of man.

Job

In the first chapter of Job there was a heavenly meeting of God and the angels.[6] What was this meeting about? What were they discussing? The Bible doesn't tell us. However, there is an implication, for when Satan joined the discussion God asked him about Job: "Hast thou considered my servant Job? for there is none like him in the earth, a perfect and an upright man, one that feareth God, and turneth away from evil."[7]

We must understand God's heart in this situation. He was deeply concerned for Job. While Job was perfect in his doing, avoiding any kind of evil, he lived apart from God. He was separated from God. The most important thing for man is his relationship with God, and Job did not have one. God and the angels must have been discussing this problem. How could they help Job?

Job's self-righteousness had conditioned him to think highly of himself. He considered himself a righteous person. In their heavenly discussion, God and the angels must have observed that Job needed to be brought low so that he could see his true inward condition and his great need of God. But who could do such a thing to Job? God could not do it. God does not plague his people. In addition, the godly angels would not do this to Job. Job had done nothing to warrant such a judgment upon him from the godly angels. So then who could render Job the help he needed?

At that point Satan entered the meeting. God phrased His question to Satan in such a way that he responded by volunteering to do to Job what had to be done. This sounds terrible. However, for Job's welfare it was absolutely necessary. Job was deluded and needed this extreme dealing to rescue him. Otherwise, he would have died apart from God.

Satan delights in causing suffering. When God seemed to exalt Job before him, Satan leapt at the chance to afflict Job. Without realizing it, Satan did exactly what was needed to help Job out of his delusion and to God.

This change in Job did not happen quickly. Job was an elderly man. His delusion was firmly grounded and deeply rooted within him. It was not something that could be easily touched.

Job was slowly worn down through all the afflictions that came upon him. However, God limited Satan. First, He did not allow Satan to touch Job personally with any kind of malady. God then told Satan that he could touch Job, but to spare his life. God's limitation of Satan assured that Job would pass through this long suffering alive.

As Job was slowly being worn down, he was changing. At first his focus was himself. But if you read the later chapters of this book, you will see that as time went on Job started seeking God. He wanted to talk with God. He wanted answers from God. He wanted to interrogate God, to put God in the witness chair and cross-examine him.

As the old Job was slowly being eroded away, worn down, consumed with disease, and dying, a new God-focused Job was coming into being. As the old self was being dissolved in the acid of affliction, Job's consciousness shifted slowly to God. As Job was experiencing the crucifixion of himself, which solved his self-righteous delusion, God maintained Job's existence. This was the practical outworking of the cross in Job's life.*

Eventually Job turned from himself to God. He stopped focusing on himself, his righteousness, his perception of his life and started seeking God. It was then that God could appear to Job. In the light and reality of God's appearing, Job finally saw himself for what he really was. Seeing God saved him from delusion; seeing God brought him into reality, destroying his delusion about himself. Then, in that light, he abhorred himself, hated himself, despised what he was, and repented.

Saul

Saul of Tarsus was a chosen vessel whom the Lord intended to use greatly. It is clear from his writings that he was an exceptionally intelligent person – one with insight and logic. He was bold and aggressive, and undeterred by fear. The Lord planned to use him not only for the spread of the gospel to the Gentiles,[8] but also to complete the divine revelation in the Bible.[9] However, Saul had a serious problem: he was greatly deluded.

Saul grew up at the feet of the Gamaliel.[10] Gamaliel was a great Jewish teacher and doctor of the law,[11] who was held in high

---

* Even though Christ had not yet been crucified, God could apply to Job the efficacy of Christ's crucifixion. God's operation is not bound by time.

esteem. He was levelheaded and wise, as seen by his handling of the confrontation between the council in Jerusalem and Peter and John.[12] Many have believed that he was a covert Christian.

Although Paul was tutored by such a sober-minded and gentle person, something happened to him when Stephen was murdered.[13] Before that time there is no record of him damaging the church in any way; after that time he was a murderer, terrorizing the believers and desiring to kill or imprison them all.[14] What happened to him when Stephen was stoned?

I believe at the time of Stephen's death the glory of God shined from Stephen's face and in Stephen's words. This attracted Saul. The glory drew him and beckoned to him. Saul was a chosen vessel,[15] and God was calling him. That shining of God's glory exposed something hidden within Saul, something dark and evil – the delusion of Judaism. God was calling Saul, but the darkness within Saul resisted. He chose the darkness and became a terrorist, a murderer, a raging madman. This is confirmed by the Lord's words[16] to Saul at the time of his conversion: "It is hard for thee to kick against the goad."* Saul had been fighting against that for which he had been chosen. In choosing the darkness, Saul became a persecutor and murderer.

Saul was trapped by and within his delusion. He was totally ignorant of his true condition. He needed to be rescued, so the Lord intervened, appeared to Saul, and surrounded him with His light.[17]

Saul was physically blinded by that encounter, which was a reflection of his true spiritual condition. He remained blind and neither ate nor drank for three days,[18] until a Christian brother named Ananias laid hands upon him and Saul received his sight.[19]

After that experience, Saul became a intrepid speaker for Christ and for God's New Testament way. He spoke forcefully for the Lord and against His opposers. He was bold, convincing others that Jesus was the Christ.

What had happened to Saul? God had saved him from the darkness of delusion within him. However, how is it that Saul was

---

* The goad was a sharp stick attached to a plow to prod livestock to keep pulling the plow.

rescued from his delusion in merely a few days, whereas Job required probably months of intense suffering to be saved? For one thing, Saul had been touched by the glory of God. He had seen Stephen's shining face, and had witnessed the gentleness and forgiveness in Stephen's response to his own martyrdom. At that time Saul had been touched in a positive way although he may not have realized it. When Jesus did appear to him on the way to Damascus, Saul called Him Lord.[20] How did Saul know this was the Lord? Because he had heard Stephen's words.[21]

For another thing, Saul was a young man unlike Job. His delusion had not yet thoroughly infected him. It had not yet had time to spread and deeply entrench itself.

In addition, Saul must have been a person of extraordinary psychological strength. Consider how much he was able to bear in his life. There have not been many men with such capacity.

Finally, consider the days of Saul's blindness. The Lord's shining upon him, his heart, and his actions must have been particularly intense. Day by day and moment by moment, Paul's delusion was being stripped away in that light. As he saw the truth, every aspect of that delusion died. It was only because of Paul's constitution and the Lord upholding and strengthening him that he was able to bear such a penetrating exposure of light. But in that light, the old Saul with his delusion died. The one who emerged was a new man, a God-regenerated man.

The Crucial Factor

Both Job and Saul were saved from delusion. What was the crucial factor in their salvation? Let us examine John 16:2-3: *yea, the hour cometh, that whosoever killeth you shall think that he offereth service unto God. And these things will they do, because they have not known the Father, nor me.*

Although the word delusion is not used by the Lord in these verses, the fact is there. The ones killing the Lord's disciples think that they are doing service to God, but they are not. In other words, they were deluded. This was exactly Saul's behavior. He also thought he was serving God by his persecution of the church.

The Lord goes on to give the reason for their delusion: *And these things they will do because they have not known the Father, nor me.* What then is the crucial factor in salvation from delusion? It is knowing Christ, knowing God.

This does not mean to know about Christ in an objective sense. Rather, it means to have a subjective, experiential knowledge of Christ. It means to experience the Father, to live in the Father's presence, and to have an intimate knowledge of His heart.

This was the crucial factor for both Job and Saul: knowing God. As God appeared and spoke with Job, His delusion dissolved. It shriveled and died in the light of God's reality. Similarly, as Paul reflected upon his experience of Christ and communed with the Lord during his days of blindness, his delusion dissipated and disappeared. Delusion and God cannot coexist. Falsehood and truth cannot coexist. When delusion is brought into God's reality, it disappears, forever dispelled by that reality.

The only salvation from delusion is God Himself *experienced*. This experience puts everything to death. Yet somehow we, his redeemed people, are raised up in resurrection to experience Him as the reality. This frees us from the delusion that ensnared, trapped, and imprisoned us.

Prayer

As we have seen in the cases of Job and Saul, salvation from delusion is exceptionally difficult. There is no easy way for us to be saved from deeply entrenched deception. The deluded person never knows they have such a condition, for if they were aware of the deception working within, they would no longer be deluded.

Furthermore, one who is deluded will invariably deny this fact. If confronted face-to-face, and told of their delusion, the response will be denial: "I am not deluded. You're the one who's deluded." There is seemingly no way to break through delusion.

However, there is something that can be done. We can kneel before the Lord in prayer, bringing our heart and mind into God, letting God touch our depths. We can beseech the Lord in prayer: "Lord, I want to know the truth whatever the cost. Have mercy and save me from all deception. Don't leave me in my pitiful condition. Whatever the cost, Lord, I want to know the truth." The Lord delights to answer such a genuine and heartfelt prayer.

Prayer affords God the opportunity for which He so longs, to save both us and others from all kinds of deception. Recall

Stephen's prayer as he was being stoned: "Lord, lay not this sin to their charge." Regarding this prayer, Augustine said that if it were not for the prayer of Stephen, Paul would not be. Stephen's prayer opened the way for God to touch Saul and save him. Genuine prayer to God avails much.[22] May we all enter into such prayer, be saved from deception of all kinds, and enter into the marvelous reality that God Himself is.

References

[1] Rom. 6:8
[2] Eph. 2:6
[3] Rom. 6:6
[4] 1 Pet. 1:3
[5] 2 Cor. 5:17
[6] Job 1:6
[7] Job 1:8
[8] Rom. 15:16
[9] Col. 1:25
[10] Acts 22:3
[11] Acts 5:34
[12] Acts 5:34-40
[13] Acts 7:54-8:1
[14] Acts 8:3; 9:1-2
[15] Acts 9:15
[16] Acts 26:14
[17] Acts 9:3; 22:6; 26:13
[18] Acts 9:9
[19] Acts 9:17-18
[20] Acts 22:8
[21] Acts 7:59-60
[22] Jam. 5:16

Appendix

The Case of James

James, the writer of the five-chapter epistle that bears his name, was the physical brother of Jesus,[1] a leading one in the church in Jerusalem[2] and an apostle.[3] In his epistle he says that his readers had heard of the patience of Job.[4] In order to understand his epistle and his reference to Job, it is necessary to understand James himself, his background, and his view and comprehension of God's move on the earth.

His Upbringing

It is clear from the New Testament that Joseph, the husband of Mary the mother of Jesus, was a law-abiding man. When Mary was pregnant with Jesus, Joseph sought to put her away privately.[5] At that time Joseph did not know about the source of Mary's child, and therefore according to the law he sought to put her way.[6] Yet he did this privately, not willing to shame Mary or expose her to any form of mistreatment. In addition, every year Joseph and Mary went up to Jerusalem to celebrate the feast of Passover,[7] which was also according to the law. This shows that Joseph and the entire household were law-keeping Jews, as practiced in the Old Testament. James grew up in this environment, and learned this practice.

He also had as his older brother the very God incarnated in Jesus. This young man lived a perfect life. He never broke the law. In fact, how could He? The law was a picture of God, and displayed His nature. For Jesus to break the law would have been for Him to do something against His own nature. This would have been impossible. As Jesus lived out the divine nature within Him, He spontaneously kept the law in every aspect. James observed the living of this God-man.

An Unbeliever

However, it is also clear that James did not see the divinity within Jesus. In fact, he was an unbeliever.[8] He provoked Christ to take some action to make Himself known.[9] He neither knew Christ in reality, nor believed.

Christ's Appearing

James remained in his state of unbelief until after Christ's resurrection. Jesus then appeared to James,[10] manifesting himself and ending James's unbelief. James required the Lord's physical appearing to believe. He was not blessed like those who have not seen and yet believe.[11] James, like Thomas, required physical evidence.

In Jerusalem

James joined the apostles in the upper room, as they prayed for the outpouring of the Holy Spirit after Christ's ascension.[12] Over time James became prominent in the church in Jerusalem, so much so that Peter considered him the leading one among the believers.[13] When Paul visited the church in Jerusalem the first time, he met only with Peter and James of the apostles.[14] At a later time, when Peter was visiting the church in Antioch, certain ones of the circumcision – that is, the Judaizers – came to Antioch to scrutinize the situation there. From Paul's wording of that event, there is the sense that they were sent to spy on Peter – they came to Antioch "from James."[15]

On Paul's last visit to Jerusalem, he went in to speak with James and the elders.[16] James pointed out the thousands of believers there, who according to him were all zealous for the law.[17] He then persuaded Paul to perform a Judaisitic ritual to impress the law-keepers that Paul still kept the law.[18] This led to Paul's long imprisonment.

His Writings

We do not know how many epistles James wrote, but God has included only one – a book of five chapters – in the New Testament. James addressed this epistle to the twelve tribes of Israel in the Dispersion. It is evident in reading this letter the James was one who practiced good works.[19] He was also one who apparently loved Proverbs, as many of his words seem to have their source in that Old Testament book.[20]

His Martyrdom

According to church history, James was martyred in Jerusalem. He was cast down from the pinnacle of the temple, stoned, and then ultimately killed with a club. In martyrdom James had a very good end.

Analysis

Taking all this into account, what can we conclude about James? He was a law-keeper from his youth. That is evident. However, he was not strong in faith. He lived with the incarnated God, and yet never recognized Him. For James to believe required the physical manifestation of Christ in resurrection. This indicates a lack of faith on James's part.

It is not stated how James rose to prominence in the church in Jerusalem. The fact that he was the physical brother of Jesus may have been a factor in his rise. It is also likely that his perfection as a law-keeper allowed him to become prominent. One who practices self-righteousness by keeping the law is attractive to those who are similarly inclined, and extremely intimidating to those who are not as versed in this practice. I imagine both of these factors played into James's standing.

On Paul's second visit to the church in Jerusalem, he was not yet an old believer. Nevertheless, those reputed to be something imparted nothing to him.[21] This certainly included James.[22] While Paul was filled with the experience and revelation of Christ, James had nothing to add to Paul. This indicates that James was not rich in Christ. While he may have been great in keeping the law, he was not great in Christ.

When those of the circumcision came down to Antioch, their very presence led Peter into dissimulation.[23] Paul rebuked him to his face because he was not living according to the truth of the gospel.[24] However, Paul tells us expressly that these came from James.[25] James sent them. We must ask why James would do this? What was James's intention? Why was he sending Judaistic, law-keeping Christians "of the circumcision" to Antioch to watch over Peter? It would seem that he wanted to keep Peter in line, behaving according to the practice of Judaism as they did in Jerusalem.

Later, when Paul came up to Jerusalem for the last time, James pointed out to him the myriad believers in Jerusalem who were zealous for the law. He was not ashamed to say this, but rather quite bold, perhaps even proud. Why were these not zealous for Christ? They were zealous for the law; what about Christ? James should have uttered these words with shamefulness. James should have realized that as the most prominent one in the church there, he had failed to bring the believers to Christ. He had led them all back into the Old Testament practice of law-keeping.

According to Paul, to whom it was given to complete the word of God,[26] Christ is the end of the law to all who believe.[27] If Christ ended the practice of keeping the law, what was James doing? What were these thousands of believers in Jerusalem doing? Why were they still in the Old Testament practice of keeping the commandments? Why hadn't they come forward into God's New Testament way of Christ being everything to the one who believes? This was not something positive. Rather it was extremely negative, showing how much James was damaging the church in Jerusalem.

Furthermore, James's suggestion for Paul to partake in the Judaistic ritual ended in Paul's long imprisonment. God would not tolerate Paul partaking of this Old Testament practice. Is this a positive matter for James? Not at all.

Consider now his epistle. He wrote it to the twelve tribes of Israel. However, in the New Testament there is neither Jew nor Greek, but Christ is *all* and in *all*.[28] In the new man, all distinction between Jews and other nationalities is gone. There is only Christ. Christ in this person, Christ in that person; Christ, Christ, Christ. There is no Jew, there is no Greek, there is no barbarian, Scythian, American, Chinese, or Italian. There is only Christ. Why would

James write to the twelve tribes? Because he had not yet entered into God's New Testament economy, God's New Testament way, His New Testament process for accomplishing His eternal purpose.

In James's epistle we see many references to good works and proverbial concepts. However, in his whole epistle of five chapters there is no mention of Christ's human life or quotation of Christ's words. He grew up with the incarnate God, and yet he tells nothing of this Person. How many words had he heard Jesus speak, and yet not one of them is in his epistle. Why wouldn't James set forth Christ before his readers? It must be that his vision was so obscured by law-keeping that he could not see.

Furthermore, in James's epistle there is no revelation from the Old Testament. Although James was versed with at least some part of the Old Testament, he displays no revelation concerning it. There is no talk of the types of Christ. There is no speaking about prophecies concerning Christ. It is as if his experience, vision, and revelation concerning Christ was nearly nonexistent. His writing is nearly devoid of God's New Testament way.

In addition, consider the book in the New Testament that precedes James – Hebrews. Paul, who almost certainly wrote this book, did so to combat all the Judaistic influences within the church in Jerusalem. Many there were falling away from the church and God's New Testament way back to Judaism. Paul wrote Hebrews to undo the enormous damage the believers in Jerusalem had undergone. He wrote it as a kind of vaccine and cure for those who had been infected by the influence of the law-keepers.

Paul wrote this after his long imprisonment, having had many years to consider the best way to combat what he saw among the believers in Jerusalem when he was there. His writing is irrefutable. He kills everything except Christ! He warns, encourages, and feeds the believers. The believers in Jerusalem had lived on milk for decades. Paul gave them solid food – meat to chew and swallow – that they might be saved from Judaism and from law-keeping.

It is no accident that the book of Hebrews precedes the book of James. This is God's placement. By such a placement God is showing what the book of Hebrews was combating. It was fighting against the damage being done by the law-keepers, the circumcision, and the Judaizers. It was fighting against the Judaistic influence so prominent in Jerusalem and so apparent in James's writing.

In Summary

What then can we say in summary concerning James? He was steeped in Judaism, legality, and the Old Testament. From his epistle we can see that he sought perfection.[29] He sought to mimic the Christ with whom he had grown up, yet without Christ Himself. That is what keeping the law is.

James was very much like Job. He appreciated Job, his perfection, and his uprightness. However, he could not see Job's difficulty, because to some degree James had the same problem. He, like the perfect Job, was a law-keeper. His focus was not on Christ, but on establishing his own righteousness and perfecting himself. He was led away from Christ.

James did not see Job's delusion of self-righteousness. Apparently, he completely overlooked the end of the book of Job, where Job says that he abhorred himself.[30] James did not see that Job lived a life apart from Christ. Recall what Job said: "I had heard of thee by the hearing of the ear; But now mine eye seeth thee." That is, I have never experienced You, seen You, communed with You before; but now I'm in touch with You. James entirely overlooked this, the most important part of the book of Job.

So, James set forth Job and his patience as an example, without realizing that Job's integrity and perfection were keeping him from God Himself. James did not see that all of this in Job had to be torn down in order for God and Job to have an intimate relationship. James's mentioning of Job's patience in his epistle was not an indication that Job was having his patience tested. Rather, it was an indication of James's poor stance with respect to God's New Testament economy.

References

[1] Gal. 1:19
[2] Acts 21:18
[3] Gal. 1:19
[4] Jam. 5:11
[5] Matt. 1:18-19
[6] Deut. 24:1
[7] Lk. 2:41
[8] Jn. 7:5
[9] Jn. 7:3-4
[10] 1 Cor. 15:7
[11] Jn. 20:29
[12] Acts 1:14
[13] Acts 12:17
[14] Gal. 1:19
[15] Gal. 2:11-13
[16] Acts 21:18
[17] Acts 21:20
[18] Acts 21:23-24
[19] Jam. 2:14, 18, 20, 24
[20] For example, Jam. 1:10-11, 12, 25; 3:2-5
[21] Gal. 2:6
[22] Gal. 2:9
[23] Gal. 2:12-13
[24] Gal. 2:11
[25] Gal. 2:12
[26] Col. 1:25
[27] Rom. 10:4
[28] Col. 3:11
[29] Jam. 1:4; 3:2
[30] Job 42:6

www.ingramcontent.com/pod-product-compliance
Lightning Source LLC
Chambersburg PA
CBHW061226070526
44584CB00029B/4002